Explaining Honour and Respect

Tom Marshall

Sovereign World

Scripture quotations are from the following versions, as indicated in the text:

NIV, New International Version. Copyright © 1973, 1978, International
Bible Society, published by Hodder and Stoughton.
ASB, American Standard Version of the Bible. Copyright © The Lockman
Foundation 1960, 1962, 1963, 1968, 1975, 1977, La Habra, California.
AV, Authorised Version.

ISBN: 1-85240-063-3

Production & Printing in England for
SOVEREIGN WORLD LIMITED
P.O. Box 17, Chichester, West Sussex PO20 6YB
by Nuprint Ltd, Station Road, Harpenden, Herts AL5 4SE.

Contents

1

The Meaning And Need For Honour

The Bible is full of strong imperatives regarding honour. Thus we are commanded to honour God (1 Samuel 2:30, Proverbs 3:9, John 5:23, 1 Timothy 6:16), our parents (Exodus 20:12, Deuteronomy 5:16, Mark 10:19), the elders (1 Timothy 5:17), our employers (1 Timothy 6:1), and the king (1 Peter 2:17). Wives are to honour their husbands (Ephesians 5:33), husbands are to honour their wives (1 Peter 3:7), and the institution of marriage is to be held in honour by all (Heb 13:4). Moreover honour is to extend to widows (1 Timothy 5:3), the elderly (Leviticus 19:2), the disadvantaged or the less successful (1 Corinthians 12:23–24), in fact, to all men (1 Peter 2:17).

In other words, what we have pictured in Scripture is an entire society built on the principle of mutual honour and respect.

What do we mean by honour?

Let us begin by defining the terms so that we know from the start what we are discussing.

Honour or respect is the recognition of a person's worth or value, and the attitude that is appropriate to that recognition.

There are two aspects to this definition that are important.

1. *Honour has to do with valuing.*

Honour recognises people as being valuable or worthy, therefore it raises the question of the value system we use to determine that worth. The way a football team assesses the worth of its players is obviously different from the way a university assesses the value of its students. In chapter 2 we will discuss the different measures of value that have to be taken into account when assessing the worth of people.

2. *Honour has to do with appropriate attitudes.*

Attitudes are different from beliefs. Beliefs are what we think about things, attitudes are not only what we think about things, but also how we feel about them and how we behave towards them. Beliefs do not often affect the way we live, attitudes always do. Beliefs involve our mind, attitudes involve our mind, our emotions and our will.

> *The Lord says: 'These people come near to me with their mouth and honour me with their lips, but their hearts are far from me. Their worship of me is made up only of rules taught by men'.* (Isaiah 29:13, NIV)

While honour always has the same meaning—the recognition of value—the attitude that is appropriate will vary with the value of the person being honoured.

God is the supreme value in the universe. To honour God therefore means to worship, glorify, exalt, reverence, magnify, praise and extol him.

Applied to human beings who are also valuable, honour means to respect, esteem, pay regard to, dignify, defer to, venerate or salute.

The importance of honour

God's commandments are always given to us for our good (Deuteronomy 10:12–13), and obedience to them is therefore the best, the most efficient and the most harmonious way for us to live. Giving honour to others is thus not only an act of obedience to God's commands, it is also vital to our mental, emotional and spiritual health, for the following reasons.

1. When I honour others I recognise how rich my life is because it is surrounded and interpenetrated by so many valuable and worthwhile people.

What is more, if people who have a regard for me and a good opinion of me, are valuable in their own right, their opinions also have value. But if I dishonour those around me, I inevitably impoverish my own life and rob it of significance because I am declaring that it is surrounded by worthless people. If the company it keeps is worthless, my life will, of necessity, also seem worthless.

2. When I am honoured I can begin to feel good about myself because my sense of my own worth and value is being affirmed.

If the society pictured in Scripture is one built on mutual honour and respect, then the society we have today is one built increasingly on dishonour. We have a barrage of dishonour in the media and in our public life, dishonouring marital faithfulness, dishonouring parents, particularly fathers, dishonouring authority and dishonouring Judaeo-Christian ethics.

In such circumstances it ought not to surprise us that so many people in our society suffer from a poor self image and feelings of worthlessness and meaninglessness. It is the inevitable result of the neglect of the biblical injunctions regarding honour. The self image is built up from the way we perceive other people relating to us, particularly the significant people in our lives. If they affirm and honour us, the chances are that we will develop a good self image, if they reject us and dishonour us, we will almost certainly acquire a poor self image. Thus if so much of the positive fabric of people's lives is persistently held up to active disrespect and honour, it is inevitable that people will begin to feel that way about themselves.

3. Honour received goes further than affecting the mind or even the emotions, it nourishes the human spirit.

We are embodied spirit and when we are honoured our life is affirmed and our spirit is strengthened. Conversely, dishonour in any of its forms such as rejection, disdain, contempt or scorn, wounds the human spirit.

> *Like a wife forsaken and grieved in spirit, even like a wife of one's youth when she is rejected.*
>
> (Isaiah 54:6, ASB)

4. Honour or respect is essential for any healthy relationship.

For any relationship whatsoever to survive and grow, four factors need to be attended to, one is love, the most rugged of the four, another is trust, the most fragile, a third is understanding, which takes longest, and the fourth is honour or respect, generally the most neglected of the four. It is virtually impossible to have a good relationship with somebody you do not respect, because the relationship seems valueless. If people in a relationship lose their respect for one another, the relationship will wither and die. By the same token, it is impossible for someone who has lost their self respect to relate well to other people, because they see themselves as valueless.

5. *Honour or dishonour affects the way we live and behave.*

A person who is honoured and knows it, has a great stake in behaving honourably, because receiving honour is so rewarding that we do not want to endanger it.

> *A good name is more desirable than great riches; to be esteemed is better than silver or gold.*
>
> (Proverbs 22:1, NIV)

But a person who is persistently dishonoured eventually sees no point in doing anything else than living down to people's evaluation of him and hence people's expectation as to how he will behave.

6. *Both honour and dishonour tend to be self-perpetuating.*

If I am honoured I will become secure in my own sense of self worth. I am then able to give honour to others and to do so genuinely and sincerely because I recognise and appreciate their value. Their being valuable and valued does not threaten my sense of my own value. Furthermore, the people I honour will in turn also become secure and free to give honour to others where honour is due.

But if I am persistently dishonoured and thus suffer from lack of self esteem I will have great difficulty in acknowledging the value of other people without feeling even more inferior and worthless myself. My attitude is more likely to be one of criticism, because I have the need to cut them down to size.

Giving content to honour or respect

Here are a cluster of words that help to fill out for us just what is meant by honour or respect.

1. Acceptance

Acceptance can be passive, a reluctant bowing to the inevitable, 'Nothing can be done about it, we will just have to accept it.' A person accepted on that basis feels merely tolerated.

Real acceptance is a much more active, positive attitude towards the person. It says in effect, 'I'm glad you are here, you make a valuable addition to this group.' A person who receives genuine acceptance in those terms feels respected and valued.

2. Affirmation

Affirmation is reinforcing a person's self worth by drawing attention to their gifts and strengths and achievements.

Affirmation is an attitude that says in effect, 'I think you are marvellous and I would like you to feel that way about yourself.'

3. Appreciation

Appreciation is more subjective, it expresses the pleasure I feel when I see you or am in your company, and my genuine delight in your successes. It says, 'I really enjoy seeing you the way you are and doing the things you do.'

4. Approval

Approval expresses my agreement with, and my commendation of, the way you behave and the things you do. It is me lining myself up on your side and saying, 'Well done. In your position I would have done exactly the same as you have done.'

5. Admiration

Admiration goes further than approval, it not only commends, it praises and looks up to the person and his or her character and achievements. It says, 'You set a standard in this that makes me want to emulate you.'

6. Acknowledgement

Acknowledgement is giving the person recogition, praise or commendation publicly or before other people, for who they are or for what they have done.

When Jesus saw Nathanael approaching, he said of him,

Here is a true Israelite in whom there is nothing false.
(John 1:47, NIV)

In all these, and in other ways, we can give substance to the words honour and respect and can learn how to express it fully and convey it in a way that has meaning.

2

Measures Of Value

If respect is the recognition of worth and value, we have to decide where value comes from, or how it arises.

Value is imputed

The first thing we have to understand is that all value is imputed, that is to say, things have value only because we give them value or ascribe value to them.

What is the value of my house?

Not what it cost to build but what someone will pay me for it. That is true about anything.

I may spend $500,000 designing and producing a super widget and then another $500,000 marketing it. If nobody will buy my widget, what is its value? Nothing, or at most, the scrap value of the materials.

On the other hand there is a piece of canvas 60cm square with paint on it. What is the value of the canvas and the paint? A few cents at most.

But if the artist who put the paint on was a Van Gogh or a Picasso, people will give a fortune to obtain it.

Value systems, measures of value

If all value is imputed, we then have to ask, What is the basis or the value system that is used for imputing value? On what grounds do we ascribe a particular value to one person and a different value to another?

Because honour has to do with recognising value, the type of people that a society honours or respects reveals very clearly the values on which the society is built. Moreover, they give us a basis for comparing our society with other societies or our society today with what it was like in other eras.

Clearly our Western society places the highest value on entertainment, sports and material wealth since it is the people who succeed in these areas who receive the most deference or honour.

But is this a legitimate value system on which to base our estimate of human beings? If not, what is the value system that ought to be used for this purpose?

The biblical value system for considering the worth of men and women has three measures of value, (1) Intrinsic value, (2) The value due to character, and (3) The value due to performance.

Intrinsic value

Intrinsic value is the value that belongs to the essence of a person or thing. For example if you have a gold ornament, you can smash it with a hammer, you can grind it to powder, you can burn it in the fire, but there is a certain value that will survive all these destructive efforts, the value of the gold metal.

That is its intrinsic value; it is irreducible, it is inalienable, it is indestructible.

13

As far as man's value is concerned, note the following important points:

1. Men and women, made in God's image, have an intrinsic value that is eternal.
They have this value because God has imputed it to them.

> *What is man that Thou rememberest him?*
> *Or the son of man that Thou art concerned about him?*
> *Thou has made him for a little while lower than the angels:*
> *Thou hast crowned him with glory and honour.*
> (Hebrews 2:6–7, ASB)

> *The precious sons of Zion,*
> *Weighed against fine gold.* (Lamentations 4:2, ASB)

Just as God has unilaterally and unconditionally given us His love, so He has unilaterally and unconditionally given us our eternal worth, and not even the fall with all its evil consequences has damaged that intrinsic value. The cross of Jesus Christ says that fallen man is still, in God's view, worth redeeming.

2. Because our intrinsic value is given to us, or imputed to us by God, it is not earned or achieved.
Indeed all our achievements do not add one iota to our eternal worth. But by the same token, because it is imputed, our eternal value is not endangered by any or all of our failures.

Thus the most destroyed or broken or devastated or handicapped human life is never a nothing. It remains eternally valuable because God has given it that value.

3. The first value that needs to be established in a child is this sense of his or her intrinsic worth, that they are valuable, and therefore acceptable, for themselves and for no other reason.
They do not have to achieve to earn it, they are not on any performance standard to merit it, they are valuable and significant in themselves. The establishment of this realisation of being intrinsically valuable is critical for the child's sense of security and belonging.

4. The existence of this intrinsic value means that we must always make a clear distinction in our mind between who the person is, and what the person does.
What the person does may be totally unacceptable in our eyes, or in God's eyes. But the person in themselves is always totally acceptable because of their intrinsic value.

Jesus always made that distinction. It always astonished me that in John 4 when Jesus said to the woman of Samaria, *'You had five husbands, and the one whom you now have is not your husband,'* the woman did not say *'Judge not that you be not judged'* or 'What business is that of yours,' she said, *'Sir, I perceive that You are a prophet.'* The reason for this response is clear. She already knew that Jesus totally accepted and honoured her as a person. Even although he knew what her lifestyle was like, he addressed her in the same terms of respect as he used when speaking to his own mother at the marriage in Cana.

The value due to character

Man was created in the image of God, that is to say he was created to reflect in his own being the moral and spiritual beauty of God's character, what the psalmist called *'the beauty of holiness.'* Therefore to God, character is everything:

He has told you, O man, what is good;
And what does the Lord require of you?
But to do justice, to love kindness,
And to walk humbly with your God. (Micah 6:8, ASB)

He who pursues righteousness and loyalty finds life,
righteousness and honour. (Proverbs 21:21, ASB)

When choosing leaders the early church always put character above charisma and virtue, or moral excellence above gift (1 Timothy 3:2–13). When Paul wrote to Timothy telling him to pass on to others the things he had heard from Paul, he did not say to clever men, or to gifted men but to faithful men, men of character (2 Timothy 2:2).

In the world today, intellectual capacity, artistic talent, technical expertise, business or political acumen, sporting and personal charisma are all rated well above character, and are sometimes held to justify the absence of moral standards in the person's actions or behaviour.

The church has succumbed sufficiently to the standards of society to downplay godly character and elevate gift and ministry. The value of character has significance for the next generation only if it is modelled in this generation, therefore it is the men and women of godly character in the church who must be honoured and held up for the next generation to emulate.

The value that is due to performance

Intrinsic value is given not earned, but the value due to character and the value due to performance are earned. Here the rule is *'honour to whom honour is due'* (Romans 13:7, ASB).

Let the elders who rule well be considered worthy of double honour, especially those who work hard at preaching and teaching. (1 Timothy 5:17, ASB)

In everything we do we need to have a commitment to excellence, at least in what we put into the task.

Whatever you do, do your work heartily, as for the Lord rather than for men; knowing that from the Lord you will receive the reward of the inheritance. It is the Lord Christ whom you serve. (Colossians 3:23, ASB)

The Bible reveals that God is also concerned with the results we achieve.

I the Lord search the heart,
I test the mind,
Even to give to each man according to his ways,
According to the results of his deeds.
(Jeremiah 17:10, AV)

Applying the measures of value

In giving honour we must be clear as to the measure of value we are using, and the person receiving honour must understand the grounds also.

(i) Intrinsic value	Given, not earned; recognises the person's eternal value.
(ii) Value due to character	Earned, not given; recognises what the person is, or has become.

17

| (iii) Value due to performance | Earned, not given; recognises what the person has done or achieved. |

A person may display outstanding talents and achievements in a particular field—the arts, sports or business, and yet display a character that is quite reprehensible. In rightly honouring their achievements we are not automatically approving or respecting their character, nor are we saying that as far as intrinsic worth is concerned they are more valuable than anyone else.

By the same token, the fact that a person's character is worthy of all respect does not entitle them to be honoured for performance that is mediocre or even inept.

Nor can a person's need to have their intrinsic worth and value emphasised be met by praising poor performance or accepting uncritically their character, lifestyle or habitual patterns of behaviour.

When we are seeking to reach those outside of Christ we must always recognise intrinsic value. Regardless of their life or lifestyle they are, and must be, totally and unreservedly accepted. It is not something you can put on or pretend; either it is true in your heart or the person will sense it. Speak to him about his sin and he will feel you are judging or condemning. But if that sense of his eternal worth is real, he will also sense that. You can then, I discover, be as straight and as plain as you need to be about his sins or his moral failures and you will 'not lose him'. He may not agree with what you say, but he will know that he is still accepted.

On the other hand he may say, 'This is me, I am a drug addict or a thief or a homosexual, you just have to accept me the way I am.' We may have to say, 'As a person I totally and completely accept you, because you are valuable to God and to me. But your lifestyle I cannot accept, because God does not accept it.'

3

How To Give Honour Or
Show Respect

It is not enough to understand the nature of honour or
respect, or even to appreciate its importance, we need to
know how to convey it. Honour has to be 'given' before the
other person can receive it, or we talk about 'paying' our
respects. Behind these expressions there is a true sense that
merely thinking respectfully about someone or just feeling
how worthy or valuable they are, is inadequate, something
has to be communicated.

Conveying honour verbally

*1. One way is simply to express it in words, in simple, sincere
statements that convey our affirmation, appreciation,
commendation or esteem.*
We can do it face to face, in which case the person can catch
the warmth in our voice and the expression on our face.
Furthermore we can amplify our meaning in a variety of
ways. Or we can do it in writing which may lack the personal
impact to some extent but is more deliberate and intentional
and gives a permanent record that the person can read over
and over again.

Whatever medium we use, we need to learn how to convey respect or honour sincerely, and how to receive it grac-
iously.

> Her children rise up and bless her
> Her husband also, and he praises her, saying:
> 'Many daughters have done excellently,
> But you excel them all'.   (Proverbs 31:28, AV)

2. Another way in which we convey honour is by speaking well of one another to third parties.

Paul did it constantly and his letters to the churches, are often full of warm personal commendation of fellow workers or colleagues.

> I commend to you our sister Phoebe, who is a deaconess of the church which is at Cenchrea: that you receive her in the Lord in a manner worthy of the saints, and that you help her in whatever matter she may have need of you; for she herself has been a helper of many, and of myself as well.   (Romans 16:1–2, ASB)

> And I rejoice over the coming of Stephanus and Fortunatus and Achaius...for they have refreshed my spirit and yours. Therefore acknowledge such men.
>   (1 Corinthians 16:17–18, ASB)

Showing honour by our behaviour

In addition to explicit expressions of respect or honour we also show it implicitly, but nevertheless clearly, by the way we behave towards one another in certain situations.

1. We convey honour by acknowledging one another in company and supporting each other in public.

For example, when we are introduced by name to a group of people and welcomed by them we sense that our significance and worth is somehow being recognised. What we feel is that we are honoured.

2. We show respect for someone when we seek their advice, or their opinions or views on a matter of concern to us, and then we treat their advice or opinions seriously.
We show that we value their opinion and at least by implication we indicate that we also respect and value them.

3. In the same way, we honour someone when we submit our views, opinions and proposals for them to critique or evaluate and when we take their views and criticisms seriously.
For example, how do you feel when the boss calls you into his office and says, 'We've made some policy changes, but before we go any further I want to run them past you. I need to know whether you think they will work or not.' You feel honoured.

4. We show regard and honour to someone when we have a genuine concern for their welfare and their best interests.
Such care says to the person that to us they are valuable and worthwhile and we want the best for them even at cost to ourselves. God says, concerning Israel:

> *Since you are precious in my sight,*
> *Since you are honoured and I love you,*
> *I will give other men in your place and other*
> *peoples in exchange for your life.*   (Isaiah 43:4, ASB)

5. Respecting or honouring people also means acknowledging their right to:

a. *Make decisions we would not make,*
b. *Make mistakes we would not make,*
c. *Hold views or opinions we do not hold, and*
d. *Follow the dictates of their own conscience.*

This is very important for the attitude of Christians towards one another, and for parents when their children grow up into adulthood.

6. It is an attitude of honour and respect towards someone when we insist on treating them as a responsible person.
Therefore we will confront them with things that are wrong or dangerous in their lives. We are saying that we consider them too valuable to allow them to spoil their lives or their testimony by not dealing with such problems, and we are prepared to risk offending them by speaking out.

7. Giving gifts can be an expression, not only of love, but also of honour.
The gift is seen as a token, or symbol of the regard we have for one another and the worth we see in one another. That is why offerings are part of our worship to God.

> *Honour the Lord with your wealth, with the firstfruits of all your crops.* (Proverbs 3:9, NIV)

So also we find Jonathan's expression of the honour in which he held David,

> *And Jonathan made a covenant with David because he loved him as himself. Jonathan took off the robe he was wearing and gave it to David, along with his tunic, and even his sword, his bow and his belt.*
> (1 Samuel 18:3–4, NIV)

8. Perhaps most important of all, we honour one another by giving ourselves to each other in relationships.
When we give ourselves to each other in friendship we are expressing our sense of the other's value and their worthiness compared with other people, because we want to have a particular place in their lives and in their affections.

Supremely in the area of relationships the sexual union of marriage confers honour.

In the marriage service we say 'With my body I thee honour.' That is why, in cases of marital infidelity, you will find in the wronged partner, deeper than any anger or hurt or grievance a feeling of having been dishonoured. Because this issue is not recognised it is rarely dealt with when counselling marriages with such problems, which is why the best intentioned attempts at reconciliation often fail.

Non-verbal ways of giving honour

We communicate in two main ways, one is verbally, that is in words, and the other is non-verbally, that is in gestures, expressions, body language, the pitch and tone of our voice and so on. Sometimes the message we communicate in words is different from the message we communicate by these latter means. Communication experts tell us that the non-verbal message is at least five times more effective than the verbal message, and if the two messages conflict the receiver will always believe the non-verbal communication. We say, 'You could tell by the way she said it she was just being sarcastic.'

Here are some of the ways in which respect or honour is communicated non-verbally. We need to pay careful attention to them because often we are not very aware of the type of non-verbal message we are sending.

1. By touch.
For example a handshake, a hug, a clap on the shoulder or a kiss on the cheek, are expressions of respect or regard. *'Greet one another with a holy kiss'* (Romans 16:16). That is why when an offered handshake is ignored, it is felt to be insulting or dishonouring.

2. By the way we look at one another.

This is behind the use of the word 'regard' in English to mean both 'to view' and 'to respect' or honouring somebody being to 'look up' to them, while 'looking down' on them is holding them in contempt.

> *Give preference to one another in honour.*
> (Romans 12:10, ASB)

> *Let each of you regard one another as more important than himself.* (Philippians 2:3, ASB)

The two things that we cannot control with our will are the tone of our voice and the look in our eyes. If we despise someone, it will show in our eyes, if we dislike them, our eyes are a giveaway. If we love someone or if we admire or respect them it will also affect the way we look at them. Jesus said, *'Your eye is the lamp of your body'* (Luke 11:34), and what is in our minds and in our hearts will show in our eyes.

3. By giving the person a particular place, a 'seat of honour' (Jeremiah 52:32) or a 'place of honour' (Luke 14:7–8).

This may be a seat at the head of the table at a meal, a seat on the platform at a public gathering or a place next to the chairman at a meeting. The spatial concept of honour also comes into the language of respect. We say of a person whom everyone holds in high regard, 'She has a special place in our estimation.'

4. By being 'present' for one another.

That is to say, being aware of and attentive to the person, and to whatever they are saying or doing. If our presence is ignored, our remarks are not responded to and the person we are speaking to has his attention elsewhere, we will feel dishonoured or treated with disrespect. But if the person puts aside what they were doing and give us their full and interested attention, we feel honoured.

5. By receiving one another.

'Receive one another' Paul says in Romans 15:7 'just as Christ also received us.' In some ways this sums up all that has gone before, it is found in a group that opens up to receive a newcomer, arms that open to embrace a returning friend, or the door of a home that opens to give entrance to a welcome guest. All express honour and respect, they say louder than words, 'You have added something of value just by coming amongst us.' Paul experienced this amongst the Galatians,

> Even though my illness was a trial to you, you did not treat me with contempt or scorn. Instead, you welcomed me as if I were an angel of God, as if I were Christ Jesus himself.   (Galatians 4:14, NIV)

4

Honour In The Family

If honour is an essential factor in all relationship it is in no place more important than in the family, because there it is first established in our lives, and there also it ought to be modelled for the next generation to learn.

Yet it is in the very familiar relationships that honour is challenged most, because living at close quarters with one another also means that you become aware of each other's weaknesses and failings. Familiarity, we are told, breeds contempt. That can be a dangerous half truth but it does underline the fact that honouring one another is not something that just happens, we have to work at it just the same as we have to work at loving one another, trusting one another and understanding one another.

Here then are some of the dynamics of honour as it affects marriage and family relationships.

1. The husband is to honour the wife.
This is given as a clear commandment to husbands.

> *You husbands likewise, live with your wives in an understanding way, as with a weaker vessel, since she is a woman, and grant her honour as a fellow-heir of the grace of life, so that your prayers may not be hindered.*
> (1 Peter 3:7, ASB)

It is very important for wives to be given honour since

many factors and many attitudes in modern society still militate against a wife's sense of self worth. For example:

a. If the wife is at home looking after the house and children she is, as far as society is concerned 'not working' or is not considered to be part of the workforce, simply because no one is paying her to do what she does.

b. If she is tending small children then, of necessity, much of her working day is spent with child level conversation, child level interests and the daily routine of housekeeping. For many young women used to the stimulus of adult interaction in a job or career this can be a difficult change to embrace.

c. The question of domain and honour is very important. Honour and dominion go hand in hand (Daniel 3:34). By domain we mean, in ordinary terms, a place of our own over which we have control and where, if we want to, we can always find privacy. Commonly the husband has his domain, his study or his workshop or his garden shed. Even the children have 'their' bedroom. Often however, the wife and mother is responsible for every room in the house but has no room of her own that is her particular domain.

d. Later in life when the children have grown up and left the home the woman faces another crisis in terms of self worth. Her mothering role has come to an end but she feels 'untrained' and inexperienced, or out of date as far as re-entering the workforce after a lengthy absence.

Husbands are therefore to live towards their wives in a way that communicates a deep honour and respect, firstly for their wife as a person of great worth and value in her own right and secondly for their wife as a wife, a covenant partner in the one flesh of marriage and as a mother, a fellow-heir of the grace of life.

There is a beautiful example of just such an honouring of a wife and mother in the description of the wife of noble character in the book of Proverbs.

Her children rise up and bless her;
Her husband also and he praises her, saying,
Many daughters have done nobly,
But you excel them all. (Proverbs 31:28, AV)

2. The wife is to honour the husband.

In the biblical teaching on marriage, when it speaks about love, the greater emphasis is given to the responsibility of the husband. There are twice as many verses that say, 'husbands love your wives' as those that say, 'wives love your husbands'.

That may be because women are responders. If they are loved they do not have much difficulty in loving in return. Nevertheless the responsibility to see that there is enough love in the marriage rests primarily on the husband.

With honour or respect on the other hand, the greater emphasis is on the wife's responsibility:

Let the wife see to it that she respect her husband.
(Ephesians 5:33, ASB)

Your own husbands...may be won...as they observe your chaste and respectful behaviour.
(1 Peter 3:1–24, ASB)

One reason for this may be that in the marketplace or the workplace the husbands self-esteem is constantly at risk. He may miss out on a sale, be passed over for promotion, be reprimanded by the foreman, or lose his job. In many cases he spends his days being told what to do, and sometimes in a boring and tedious routine.

A wife can reinforce and restore a husband's sense of self worth better than anyone else in his life—or she can devastate it more effectively than anyone else because she knows his real weaknesses and his points of failure. The greatest gift a wife can give to her husband is for him to have the realisation that he is honoured, esteemed and admired by the woman he loves most of all in the world.

3. Children are to honour their parents.

God's requirement that we honour our father and mother is the fifth commandment in the Decalogue.

> *Honour your father and your mother, as the Lord your God commanded you, that your days may be pro-longed, and that it may go well with you in the land which the Lord your God gives you.*
>
> (Deuteronomy 5:16, ASB)

In Ephesians 6:2 it is called *'the first commandment with a promise'* because God has declared specific blessings for those who obey it. The blessings of long life *(that your days may be prolonged)* and prosperity *(that it may go well with you on the land)*. Moreover the importance God places on this duty is seen by the fact that the commandment is repeated explicitly at least ten times in Scripture (Exodus 20:12, Deuteronomy 5:16, Leviticus 19:3, Matthew 15:4,6, Matthew 19:19, Mark 7:10, 10:19, Luke 18:20, Ephesians 6:2), besides other numerous references to the subject. In one instance (Leviticus 19:3), the order of the parents is reversed, *'Every one of you shall reverence his mother and his father.'*

Note the following important points:

a. Obedience to parents belongs to our childhood, it comes to an end in adulthood when we take responsibility for our own lives. *Honouring parents however, is a life long duty and responsibility.*

b. Training in honouring begins in childhood; fathers have to train the children to honour and respect their mother, and mothers have to train the children to honour and respect their father. But children learn by modelling and therefore

29

they need to see the parents respecting and honouring each other.

c. When we honour our parents we are honouring the role that they filled in our lives. Our fathers gave us life, in other words, he begot us. Our mother carried us in the womb for nine months and nurtured our early existence. For the value of these contributions our parents are to be honoured, whether they were good parents or mediocre parents or bad parents.

d. When we honour our parents in the role they fulfilled in our lives we are honouring the Fatherhood of God, 'the Father from whom every family in heaven and on earth derives its name' (Ephesians 3:14). In Scripture a name means, not just a form of address but an identity. Paul is saying that every human family is in a measure a derivative of God's eternal Fatherhood. Therefore when we dishonour our parents we dishonour what stands behind their parenthood, the Fatherhood of God.

This is the reason behind the requirement of death for the one who curses his father or mother (Exodus 21:17, Leviticus 20:9, Matthew 15:4). To this day, cursing parents, that is speaking malevolently against them, can bring deadly repercussions in the lives of those who sin in this way.

e. Today society is reaping the results of a generation or generations of parents who have not trained their children to honour their parents. The result is that on the one hand the wisdom of the past generation has not been passed on to the younger generation because it has not been respected, and on the other hand, aged parents are shunted off into a nursing home because they are an encumbrance rather than a treasured part of the family inheritance.

4. Parents are to honour their children.
Every child is born with two created needs, the need for love and the need for significance. Significance has to do with

honour, and the giving of honour to the child is part of what it means to father him or her. In fact, the distinction between mothering and fathering may be that mother substantially meets the child's need for love and father substantially meets the child's needs for worth. Of course both must love and both must honour but the chances are that when a small child falls over and hurts itself, it is mother he or she runs to for comfort, but if they come home from school with a drawing they are quite proud of, it is father they want to show it to.

Certainly in the significant times in the life of Jesus you find the Father breaking the silence of heaven to affirm and honour the Son.

> *and behold, a voice out of heaven saying, 'This is my beloved Son in whom I am well pleased'.*
> (Matthew 3:17, ASB)

> *Then a cloud formed, overshadowing them, and a voice came out of the cloud, 'This is my beloved Son, listen to him'.* (Mark 9:7, ASB)

> *For not even the Father judges any one, but he has given all judgement to the Son, in order that all may honour the Son even as they honour the Father.*
> (John 5:22–23, ASB)

Here are the important points regarding honour as far as children are concerned.

a. A child's intrinsic value must be emphasised first of all, that he is valuable for who he is not for what he does. This cannot be over emphasised. Only when children are secure in their sense of being accepted and being valued for themselves, can they be challenged to earn the honour that can be achieved by performance. Otherwise they will grow up in the belief that their parents' acceptance, and thus also their

31

parents' love, have to be earned. Then you get the performance-driven child, who grows up into an adult haunted by a perpetual sense of insecurity, or the child who despairs of ever making the grade with their parents and becomes a bitter rebel.

b. The value due to character is also a critical part of the training of children if they are to grow up to be honourable men and women. Telling the truth, being fair, keeping promises, being loyal, not cheating, being polite and having a sense of duty are all qualities and principles that children must be trained to live by, and to live by because they produce character and character is what is supremely valuable. Therefore children must be able to see these principles modelled in the lives of their parents and see character being admired and honoured by them.

c. Children must also be brought up to appreciate the honour that is given to performance, and to be encouraged to pursue it. In the beginning wise parents reward intention rather than achievement, and effort rather than success, but as the child grows, standards of achievement need to be set, so that the child learns the satisfaction of earning recognition and reward for work well done.

But it does nothing for children to be given praise for work that they know is careless and sloppy or where they did not really try. That will not reassure them of their value for themselves, nor will it encourage them to try to improve their performance next time.

d. Finally discipline has an important part to play in honour. Good parents discipline their children because they consider them too valuable to waste. Children respect parents who discipline them fairly because in their hearts they recognise that their father and mother are being true parents. To let children get away with things they know are wrong robs them of the ability to feel good about themselves. In a word it is dishonouring. The writer to the Hebrews elaborates on this very point.

> *Endure hardship as discipline; God is treating you as sons. For what son is not disciplined by his father? If you are not disciplined [and everyone undergoes discipline] then you are illegitimate children and not true sons. Moreover we have all had human fathers who disciplined us and we respected them for it.*
>
> (Hebrews 12:7–9, NIV)

Mutual honour within the family reinforces family life, because it says more clearly than anything else, 'This family is incredibly valuable because it is made up of such incredibly valuable people.' It has nothing to do with material possessions or the so-called standard of living. It has everything to do with personal worth and the valuing of relationships. It heals and supports children against the hurts to their self confidence and the blows to their dignity that they experience in the world around them, and it gives them a secure base from which to have the courage to attempt great things, and if they fail, to find the courage to try again.

Lack of mutual honour in the family has weakened it, sometimes fatally, against the negative influences that today try to destroy it. Only those who see the family as a worthless institution, perhaps because they have experienced it as such, will fall for the theories of the social engineers who think they can replace it with something better.

5

Honour In Business, Church And Community

Most of the vocational and social relationships we form are within organisations in which people are divided into two distinct groups, one of which has more power, authority and influence than the other. For example, we have employers and employees, managers and workers, ministers and congregations, leaders and followers. The question of mutual honour and respect is of vital importance in all these relationships but is often grossly neglected or misunderstood in the following ways:

1. Those with positions of leadership or control assume that they are automatically entitled to respect and honour by virtue of their office.
They take it for granted as one of their natural and inalienable rights, with no thought that they have to earn it and can easily lose it.

2. Often managers or leaders tend to look down on those they lead, or those whose futures they control, as being somehow inferior or less valuable than themselves.
The status loaded language that surrounds management and leadership is used to reinforce this distance. For example, managers and leaders are 'superiors', the others are 'subordinates'; orders 'come down' from the top and to gain a management position is 'promotion'.

3. Those who are employed or managed or led have the reverse problem, they struggle often against the feeling of not being respected or honoured, of being 'used' as though they were mere machines or tools or production units.

It is likely in fact, that very many of our industrial disputes are not over money or working conditions at all, but over respect. The sense amongst workers is, 'If they are going to treat us like machines, and we have to put up with that sort of treatment, then they are going to have to pay for it.'

The biblical injunctions regarding respect and honour, apply even-handedly to both master and servant. Honour and respect is due by each to the other.

> *Slaves, obey your earthly masters with respect and fear, and with sincerity of heart, just as you would obey Christ. Obey them not only to win their favour when their eye is on you, but like slaves of Christ, doing the will of God from the heart.*
>
> *Serve wholeheartedly, as if you were serving the Lord, not men, because you know that the Lord will reward everyone for whatever good he does, whether he is slave or free.*
>
> *And masters, treat your slaves in the same way. Do not threaten them, since you know that he who is both their Master and yours is in heaven, and there is no favouritism with him.* (Ephesians 6:5–9, NIV)

Leaders, and respect for their people

By virtue of their position, leaders in any field of activity tend to move in different circles to their people, and have certain advantages over them. They go to meetings their people do not go to, they have access to information their people are not privy to, and they meet other leaders their people do not meet. All these things can distance leaders from their people, so that they 'lose the common touch.' When they have lost touch with the people, they are no longer leading them.

But when leaders honour their people they enhance their own stature because they are making a statement that says, 'This is a valuable function for me to lead because it is staffed by such very worthwhile people.'

Here are some of the important ways for management, and indeed all leadership, to ensure that in the workplace they treat their people with respect and honour.

1. People are to be recognised as valuable and worthwhile in their own right.

As a consequence,

a. The needs and concerns of people are not to be sacrificed to corporate goals or ends.

b. Every endeavour is to be made to match jobs to people's strengths so that they get fulfilment and satisfaction from their work.

c. Every person is to be given encouragement, opportunity and assistance to develop their potential and advance their chosen career.

d. Every person should be recognised, known by name, spoken to courteously and treated fairly and considerately by their immediate superiors.

2. People's efforts should be adequately recognised.

a. It is important that people receive sincere thanks, commendation and praise from those they serve of those who are in authority over them. It is very easy for management to think, 'Well that is what he is paid to do anyway,' or 'She is just doing her job.' It is as important for people to be appreciated and affirmed as it is for them to be adequately paid.

b. Because leaders are generally given a kind of representative status they are often the ones who are singled out to receive the praise and commendation and sometimes personal advancement when their team or department has performed well. They must be careful to give honour where honour is due and to acknowledge publicly the work of the team that produced the results.

3. People's views and opinions should be sought and taken into account in matters that affect them.

The views of the people who will have to implement a policy should always be sought beforehand, not only because they may have something useful to add, but as a matter of courtesy or respect. But this kind of feedback will be reliable only when the people are sure that the leaders,

a. Really want to know what they think,

b. Will treat their opinions seriously and with respect and,

c. Will not hold it against them if they criticise, or do not agree with the leaders' views.

4. People are given the reasons for management decisions that affect them.

Where management or leaders make decisions that affect people, then, even if they have been consulted, the reasons for the decisions should be explained fully to them.

If merely the bare decision is released, the message also being communicated to the people is that their views were not thought to be important enough to be considered, or that they themselves are not clever enough to understand the reasonings of management or leadership.

5. Leaders should take their people into their confidence.
This is an aspect of trust but it is also a mark of respect where leaders recognise that the people involved in any organisation or activity have a right to know what is going on. In particular leaders honour their people by sharing the bad news with them as well as the good news, because what they are saying thereby is that they recognise the people as having the qualities of courage and strength of character to face difficult and taxing circumstances without losing heart.

6. Leaders honour their people by setting them high standards and expecting superior effort and performance from them.
The converse of this is that they also show respect for their people by not letting them get away with work or output that is well below their real capacity. When a worker's shoddy or half hearted efforts are overlooked, what is being communicated is that poor quality or inferior workmanship is all that can be expected from him and he is not worth the effort of trying to train him to do better.

This is an important example of the necessity of making a difference between who the person is and what the person does. The superior should be able to say to the worker, 'Look, I value you as a member of this team and I don't want to lose you. But this standard of performance I can't accept and because I know you can do better, I won't accept it. Let's see what we can do to remedy the situation.'

Respect for leaders

The respect that is due to leaders because of their character and performance is everywhere enjoined in Scripture.

> *Now we ask you, brothers, to respect those who work hard among you, who are over you in the Lord and who*

admonish you. Hold them in the highest regard in love because of their work. (1 Thessalonians 5:12–13, NIV)

When people honour and respect their leaders they enhance their own roles and standing because they are recognising that they are being led by valuable and worthy leaders. Conversely, disrespect for leaders erodes the self respect of the group.

Note the following important points:

1. In honouring the leader, one of the values that is being recognised is the value due to performance, specifically the way he performs as a leader.
The essential task of the leader is always to deal with the future, that is,

a. To set goals and objectives for the organisation or team,

b. To guide the team towards reaching those goals, or attaining the objectives, and

c. To handle the difficulties and problems that stand in the way of reaching those goals.

No matter how able the leader is in other areas, if he is incompetent in these leadership functions he will be in danger of losing the people's respect for him as a leader, no matter how much they may respect him as a person.

2. The second important value that is being recognised is that of character.
People respect leaders who care for their welfare, who are fair and just, who are honest and truthful in their dealings with them, who stand up for them, and who show courage and resolve in the face of problems and difficulties.

3. The particular ways in which people honour their leaders include the following:

a. By the readiness, willingness and cheerfulness with which their instructions are received and obeyed, and by the manner in which duties are carried out.

b. By the way in which people refer to their leaders in public, identify themselves with the leaders, and claim a kind of 'ownership' over them. They talk with a certain pride about 'our' boss, 'our' foreman or manager or minister or captain.

c. By the readiness with which they accept the fact that the leaders by virtue of their position may have certain privileges because they carry certain responsibilities.

d. By the extent to which they model themselves on certain admired qualities of the leaders or make the particular achievements of the leaders the kind of things they themselves aspire to attain.

6

Things That Damage Respect Or Make Honouring Difficult

As well as knowing how to recognise value in people and the appropriate ways to convey that appreciation, we need to understand the things that militate against respect and honour, so that we can avoid them or correct them.

We can deal with the subject from two aspects, firstly the things that make it difficult for other people to respect us, and secondly the actions or attitudes we may have that are dishonouring towards others.

Things that make it difficult for people to respect us

1. Inadequacy, incompetence or repeated failure.

Failure does not of itself endanger other people's respect for us or even our own self respect. The simple truth is that we were all created to be good at some things but not good at everything. Success in life comes from knowing what you are gifted to do well and then expending all your efforts at getting better and better at what you are already good at doing. In other words we should develop our strengths rather than concentrate all our efforts at trying to improve our weak areas.

Inadequacy or failure will however cause us to lose people's respect, when:

a. It is shown in areas where we have claimed to be competent.

For example, I am not likely to lose people's respect because I am no good at map reading. But if I claim to be proficient at map reading and lead a tramping party into the bush only to get thoroughly lost, I am likely to lose their respect for me as a guide quite rapidly.

b. *It is in an area that is essential to the task I have to undertake.* A person in a leadership role may have a very wide range of capabilities but if he or she lacks the ability to lead they will soon lose people's respect for them as leaders although people may still have a deep respect for their technical ability or regard for them as a person.

c. *It is clear that failure is due to lack of effort.* If we give a situation our very best shots but still fail, we are unlikely to lose people's respect. They will say, 'Well, at least he tried hard.' But if our efforts are usually half hearted or perfunctory people are going to find it difficult to have respect for them.

2. Irresponsibility
When a person seeks to gratify his own desires with no thought of the consequences of his behaviour, particularly the affect his actions have on other people, his conduct is irresponsible and will generally be held to be dishonourable.

Similarly when a person, particularly one in leadership, seeks to evade responsibility for the consequences of his actions or decisions by 'passing the buck' or blaming somebody else, he soon loses people's respect.

3. Selfishness
In all the studies of man's history there has never been any evidence of any human society that has admired the selfish person. Some have admired the proud man, the cruel man, the crafty man, even the treacherous man, but never the selfish man. Selfishness and self seeking, particularly when a

person uses his position as leader to accomplish his own ends rapidly lowers him in people's estimation.

4. Self indulgence and self pity.

There is a certain reluctant admiration sometimes for the strong self sins like pride and arrogance, but never for the weak self sins like self indulgence and self pity. They are seen as particularly reprehensible in leaders who are soft on themselves, take advantage of their position to avoid the discomforts and hardships that their people have to go through, or who bemoan their lot and fall prey to the 'poor me' syndrome when the going gets tough. It is in the bad times that leaders are really needed and there is an intuitive feelings that leaders should understand that and ought to rise to the occasion when difficulties and problems have to be faced.

5. Moral failure

Here we are not speaking about the fallenness with which all of us are tainted and against which the very best of Christians still have to strive. But there are some areas of moral failure that we consider particularly dishonourable, particularly in leaders or those who hold positions of prominence or responsibility. They include:

a. Moral weakness or the inability to stand up under pressure. This is seen when we abandon our stated principles because of opposition, or in order to protect ourselves, or because keeping them is too costly. Conversely we respect anybody who has the courage of their convictions.

b. Disloyalty or betrayal. Disloyalty is abandoning those to whom we are committed or to whom we owe support or assistance. Betrayal is doing the same kind of thing but doing it for our personal advantage. That is what distinguished the sin of Judas from that of Peter. Peter abandoned Jesus out of fear, Judas abandoned him for 30 pieces of silver, the one was disloyalty, the other was betrayal.

c. Breaking promises, particularly serious vows where we pledge our word, for example, marriage vows, or encouraging or tempting someone to break such vows.

Keeping one's promises, even when inconvenient or costly was once a matter of honour. We still say, 'Word of honour' or we 'honour' our undertakings or obligations. Thus breaking our word is not only a breach of trust, it is a slight on our honour.

d. Dishonesty and all forms of deceitful, fradulent or hypocritical behaviour.

e. Unfairness, injustice, partiality and favouritism, particularly when committed by people who are in positions of power or leadership or who do it for personal gain or advantage.

f. Meanness, pettiness, sulkiness and smallmindedness in all their forms are sure ways to lose people's respect. Similarly, the person who cannot take a joke against themselves, is not big enough to admit a mistake or apologise when he finds himself in the wrong, or gets offended at the slightest criticism, will never retain people's respect.

Attitudes that are dishonouring towards the other person

1. Criticism, nagging and fault finding
There are obviously times when a person or a person's work has to be evaluated and things that are wrong or inadequate have to be pointed out. But a constant attitude of fault finding, belittlement and the harping on defects or imperfections in performance or behaviour, is very destructive of a person's self confidence and sense of self worth, particularly in the case of children.

Where errors have been made, a very different personal message is communicated when we ask, 'What went wrong?' than when we say, 'What have you done wrong?'

2. Discourteous and disrespectful speech and behaviour in all its forms.

It is particularly blameworthy because it is particularly hurtful when rude, careless or demeaning speech or attitudes are expressed towards those who are least able to defend themselves. For example, the poor, the elderly, the young or the helpless.

3. Embarrassing the other person, or putting them down in public.

Humour can be delightful, not only laughing with one another but sometimes laughing at one another. But there is also a barbed and belittling kind of humour that is at the other person's expense because it holds them up to ridicule over things to which they are known to be sensitive. It can also be a way of getting at people and then avoiding responsibility for the hurt and embarrassment by protesting, 'It was only a joke.'

4. Parading the other person's failures or weaknesses in public or before others.

There is great wisdom, as well as great courtesy, in the biblical injunction,

> If your brother sins against you, go and show him his fault just between the two of you. (Matthew 18:15, NIV)

Where people have to be corrected or their mistakes pointed out, it should always be done in private. There is a far better likelihood of getting improved results when you seek to protect the person's self esteem even when you have to deal very directly with his failures.

5. *Talking down to people or treating them as incompetent.*

This is the disparaging attitude that either refuses to explain or discuss a matter with people because they are not considered clever enough, or educated enough to understand, or else goes into over elaborate and pedantic explanations of simple matters to indicate the level of intelligence of the hearers.

6. *Domination or manipulation*

All forms of domination, manipulation, or exploitation are demeaning because they regard people as merely things to be used or as expendable means for leaders to achieve their private ends or private ambitions. This can be a great danger for very task oriented leaders, whose one aim is to achieve their goals at any cost. Their people may struggle to remain committed but end up feeling 'used'. People in any relationship who feel used, feel that they have been dishonoured.

7. *Ignoring people or disregarding their rights.*

Ignoring or overlooking people is the classic sin of omission as far as honour is concerned, because it says by implication that they are not worth bothering with.

The same is true of the management or leadership insensitivity that disregards people's rights, is thoughtless about inconveniencing them, or inconsiderate of their welfare and never bothers to thank them for any service they render or things they do.

In all the above ways, and in others, disrespect and dishonour can be communicated. Sometimes it is deliberate and overt or done openly; sometimes it is deliberate but covert or underhand; and sometimes it is done unconsciously. The message of dishonour however, whether explicit or implicit is always damaging and often devastating because it calls into question the value and worth, and the sense of significance of those towards whom it is directed.

7

Restoring Lost Respect, Recovering Honour

When people in a relationship lose respect for one another, the relationship is in great danger of being irreparably damaged. The reason for this is that if respect is lost, the relationship itself loses all value, and there will be little motivation for either of the parties to try to save it or attempt to restore it.

There are three possible questions to be answered

1. When a person has lost the respect of people, how can he regain it?
2. When people have lost respect for a person or a group, how can it be restored?
3. When a person has lost all self respect, can it be recovered, and if so, how?

What measures of value are involved?

The key to understanding the restoration of respect and honour goes back to its nature as the recognition of worth or value (see Chapter 1), and the three different measures of value on which that recognition is based (see Chapter 2).

To know what has to be done in any particular situation

depends on first understanding the nature of the value that has been damaged or lost, that is, whether it was:

1. Intrinsic value
2. Value due to character, or
3. Value due to performance.

The process of recovery or restoration will differ in each case.

1. Recovering intrinsic value

Because a person's intrinsic value is given or imputed to him by God, it can neither be lost or damaged. Even when a person has failed so totally that all value due to performance is gone, and even when his habitual pattern of behaviour has been so evil that all value due to character has been lost, his intrinsic worth as a human being made in God's image remains, because it is given or imputed to him by God.

Nevertheless we may lose, or indeed never have had, the sense of our own, or other people's intrinsic worth. And when we do not have that sense of worth and significance, nothing we possess, accomplish or achieve can substitute for it.

Restoration or discovery of a person's intrinsic value takes place at the Cross.

The death of Jesus is God's final statement that man, even in his fallen state, is still, in God's view, worth redeeming at the price of his beloved Son. That is the ultimate honour conferred on humankind, the ultimate valuation against which all our attitudes and actions towards people are to be judged.

The highest honour Paul could give a man was, *'A brother for whom Christ died'* (1 Corinthians 8:11). For such a man, even a weak brother, Paul would do anything. If eating meat caused such a one to stumble, Paul would be a vegetarian till the day he died; he would live by the weak brother's conscience not his own because he would not cause problems for a person of such value, a brother for whom Christ died.

But the intrinsic value imputed to man by God is a spiritual valuation, therefore 'knowing' it is a revelation that comes through the Holy Spirit.
It is one thing to understand the concept with our mind, it is a totally different thing to 'know' it by the illumination of the Holy Spirit.

> *We have not received the spirit of the world but the Spirit who is from God, that we may understand what God has freely given us.* (1 Corinthians 2:12)

Once we have 'seen' this, we have a benchmark below which our value, and any person's value can never fall, and above which it can never rise. It is the corrective against pride when we succeed because we realise all our achievements add nothing to this value, it is our security against despair when we fail because we realise that our failures do not endanger this value. It means we need never be overawed or cowed by any person no matter how exalted they are in the eyes of the world, and we can never look down on any person no matter how handicapped or ignorant or base they may be. It is at this level that we are the objects of redemption, and received by God.

> *To the praise of the glory of his grace, wherein he has made us accepted in the beloved.* (Ephesians 1:6, AV)

Thus at the cross ultimate honour was injected as it were into the bloodstream of the human race with the capacity to recover and restore respect and honour after it has seemingly been lost beyond recovery or devastated beyond repair. Meeting at the cross we begin to see each other through the eyes of Christ, to see each other bearing the

49

honour bestowed by Christ, a brother or a sister for whom Christ died.

2. The value due to character
The value due to character is earned, not given (1 Corinthians 16:18), *therefore it can be damaged or lost altogether.* Generally we lose respect for a person because there is persistent and habitual failure to act rightly in one or more moral areas that are vital to the relationship or are particularly important to us. For respect to be regained, the following steps will have to be taken by the person concerned.

1. Repentance
This is more than an apology or an expression of regret for what has happened. It requires,

a. A clear understanding on the part of the offending party as to what has occurred and what is to be done about it.

b. A sincere acknowledgement that the law of God has been broken, that it is a righteous law and that it was wrong to break it.

c. A genuine acknowledgement of personal guilt in breaking the law, with no excuses or rationalisations.

d. A sincere intention to amend and to be obedient in the future to the law that has been broken.

2. Forgiveness
There must be a request for forgiveness and with it faith that the offended party:

a. Is willing to forgive, and does so, but

b. Still preserves a true regard for the law of God that has been broken. In other words the offer of repentance must never be dismissed with, 'It doesn't matter'.

3. Restitution

This is not earning forgiveness, nor is it punishment, but it is making amends for the wrongs done and thus restoring shalom and relationship. What ought to be done, or what would be appropriate restitution should be mutually agreed between the parties.

4. Reordering

This is the willingness by the person who has failed to spend time rebuilding the part of their character that has proved to be seriously flawed. It may involve strategies to change dangerous or unhelpful behaviour patterns or ministry for emotional healing or to break bondages or hindrances.

There also has to be a realisation that character building is a slow process and therefore the willingness to allow time for God's governmental dealings in the person's life and for the person to develop confidence in those areas in which he has so often failed before. We can honour a person for the sincerity of his repentance and his willingness to make amends, but we want to be able to go on and honour him for what he has become in the process of change.

There is at such a time in a person's life a real need for a spiritual friend or mentor who can give support and encouragement and recognise the progress that is made, but who remains objective enough to resist impatience and insist on the job being done properly.

3. The value due to performance

When respect has been lost in these circumstances, generally no question of moral censure or blame arises, and respect for the person's character may be unaltered. Nevertheless, there have been serious inadequacies, repeated mistakes and irretrievable errors in judgement so that people have lost all confidence in the person's ability to function in the role he is in.

In dealing with the situation, there is need for wisdom and

compassion so that potentially useful lives and ministries are not shipwrecked. The steps that need to be undertaken for restoration are as follows:

1. Analysis
There should be a careful analysis of the nature of the failure or failures and more importantly, the reasons for them.

a. It may be that the person is in the wrong position, and what is involved is a case of job mis-match. For example, a person who is not a leader but is in a leadership role will find it a high stress occupation that demands things he cannot give.

b. The person may be out of his depth, that is, although he has the right kinds of ability, he faces situations beyond his knowledge or experience or skill to handle.

Analysis requires insight and honesty and humility on the part of the person who has failed to accept the findings.

2. Restoration
The process of restoring people wounded by such failures involves,

a. Helping them to understand the reasons for their failure so that they are released from feelings of guilt.

b. Reinforcing their sense of self worth (intrinsic value) by the reassurance of people genuinely accepting and valuing them as persons.

c. Obtaining an accurate picture of the person's strengths and motivations so that they can be helped to get launched in an area that suits their gifts.

d. Making plans to deal with inadequacies, perhaps by moving the person back to a level more in keeping with their ability and experience so that self confidence can be restored.

e. Providing on-going pastoral care including attention to other areas of the person's life that may have been affected by the failure, for example his wife and family.

f. Where the failure has affected other people or an organisation, there may be the need for a strategy to be developed to deal with the immediate and long term consequences so that the position can be retrieved if possible, and the failure corrected.

Finally wrong feelings and critical attitudes should be put right on both sides. This is particularly important when a person has failed in a leadership position.